By Gary Beck

Novels

Extreme Change
Acts of Defiance
Flawed Connections
Call to Valor
Sudden Conflicts
Crumbling Ramparts

Flare UP
Raise High the Walls
Still Defiant
State of Rage
Wave Length
Protective Agency

Poetry

Expectations
Days of Destruction
Dawn in Cities
Assault on Nature
Songs of a Clerk
Civilized Ways
Conditioned Response
Displays
Resonance
Perceptions
Fault Lines
Tremors
Virtual Living
Perturbations
Blossoms of Decay

Rude Awakenings
Blunt Force
The Remission of Order
Contusions
Transitions
Earth Links
Mortal Coil
Desperate Seeker
Too Harsh For Pastels
Temporal Dreams
Severance
Redemption Value
Fractional Disorder
Disruptions
Ignition Point

Play Collections
The Big Match and other one act plays
Collected Plays of Gary Beck Volume I
Plays of Aristophanes translated then directed by Gary Beck

Short Story Collections
A Glimpse of Youth
Now I Accuse and other stories
Dogs Don't Send Flowers and other stories

Essays
Collected Essays of Gary Beck

Ignition Point

Gary Beck

To Tom Sheehan, a resonating voice of clarity in an age of academic propensities. Your pleasure in writing is an example for all of us.
Best always,
Gary

Poems from Ignition Point have been published in:

Antarctica Journal, BlogNostics, Cacti Fur, Conceit Magazine, Contemporary Literary Review India (CLRI), Dead Snakes, Dissident Voice, El Portal, Eskimo Pie, Eye on Life Magazine, Flytrap Uprising (Blue Spider Press), Fresh! Literary Magazine, In Between Hangovers, In Parentheses. Jellyfish Whispers (Kind of a Hurricane Press), Penumbra Art and Literary Journal, Poetic Diversity, Poetry Space, Straight Forward Poetry, Taj Mahal Review (Cyberwit), The Broad River Review, The Magnolia Review, The Screech Owl, The Vehicle, TreeHouse, Walking is Still Honest Press, Winamop Magazine, Writer's Block Magazine, Ygdrasil Journal, Your One Phone Call.

Contents

A Gentler Age

A pretty young woman
crossed a city street
skipping, frolicking,
possibly listening to music
on her headset.
At first I thought she was happy,
then I thought she was stoned,
then I wondered idly
if she was demented.
At least I didn't suspect
she was demonic,
a sign of progress
since burning the possessed.

Lost Leaves

Winter rules,
willows are not weeping
saving green tears for spring
seeking invisibility
to conceal rude nakedness.
No one notices bare limbs,
hears sighs of relief
that tree shame is ignored.

Bird Watching

In order to see birds
you gotta look,
especially in cities
if you want to see real birds,
not pigeons,
the closest birds to man
in urban confinement,
waiting to be the vector
of avian flu
infecting the future;
not just sparrows,
aggressive gangsters
reproducing like….
eliminating finches, bluebirds,
whoever can't compete,
not tough enough
to fight for a place
on the feeders.
But if you're patient,
keep looking,
you'll see cardinals, blue jays, robins,
the diva mockingbird
singing nature's songs,
ignored by most of us,
easily drowned out
by machine snarls
that serenade our days.

Commuter Time

I waited in the rain
for a carriage
for almost two hours
to take me home
after a long day.

I waited in the rain
for a streetcar
for almost an hour
to take me home
after a long day.

I waited in the rain
for a bus
for almost thirty minutes
to take me home
after a long day.

I wonder how long
my children will wait
since a hundred years
of progress
doesn't move us much faster.

Torn

I stand in the rain
pouring down on my head,
washing away
tears of rage,
as I watch
my ex-girlfriend's window,
hoping to see her once more.
I can't make up my mind
whether to keep watching,
or go home
and get my pistol.

Non-Scientific Inquiry

I do not know
if I'll return
after death
in human form,
the wheel of fate
making its turn.
Heaven or hell
has no allure,
beyond my comprehension
how human institutions
resemble imagined creations.
Resurrection alien
to my limited biology,
almost as foreign
as nothingness,
a concept not in my sphere.
So when I die
there will be something new,
or non-existence,
leaving one conclusion,
to better use
the time I have.

Seasonal Difference

As the days get warmer
skirts get shorter
baring tantalizing flesh
to those who care to look,
abundant protein,
tolerant customs,
enriches westerners,
alienates Muslims.

The Last Blossom

A row of Magnolia trees
bloomed briefly,
exquisite flowers,
intoxicating scent,
unnoticed
by most New Yorkers
busily intent
on their affairs,
city dwellers
more and more unaware
of what is near them
rarely looking up or down,
even more dangerous,
not looking around.
As we further detach ourselves
from impending reality
it's unreasonable to expect
perception of nature's wonders,
now a row of green trees,
like other green trees,
except for one blossom,
soon to fall.

Urban Passage

Streets of strife
disrupt security,
the last serenity
of city dwellers
dwindling morally,
having lost the thread,
the throbbing pulse
that welds together
diverse strains
huddling tightly
in cramped spaces,
insufficient
to allow rampages
to disrupt practices
that bring us
out of constriction.

Reckonings

What I have done
that affected others
with pain and suffering
was never meant
with evil intent,
just acts of blindness,
thoughtlessness,
non-consideration
of the needs of others,
carelessly abandoned
to whatever fate
I do not know,
self-punishment
no remedy
for wrong actions,
a daily reminder
there is no forgiveness
for cruel behavior.

Ordinary

Birds do not have
        cities,
    indoor plumbing,
        philosophy,
surviving
        mostly by chance.
    Nature's selection,
    human intervention,
    combine
            to interfere
    with normal function.

Descent

I seek high places,
    soul adrift
    in the suppuration
    of silence,
parting clouds of sorrow
painting sterile landscapes,
sad lamentations for yesterdays,
    squandered
    in porous pursuits
    discovering danger
    in this ravaged land
of material appetite,
    inundating
    diminishing icebergs
crowded with sea creatures
    no longer singing
    beast songs,
        throttled
    by the crush of man
sucking the juices
    from a weary land,
    once fertile loins closing,
        denying
sweet intercourse,
    no longer devoted
        to reproduction,
removing responsibility
    for dwindling tomorrows.

Accelerated Horror

The news of the day
tries harder and harder
to shock us
with horrible events,
progressively straining
boundaries of morality,
some crimes so terrible
terrorism seems more natural
by comparison,
since at least we understand
the nature of hate.

Direct Current

Courtesy is a stream
flowing downhill
gathering force,
effecting change,
softening reality
abrading the kindness
necessary for survival
of congested city dwellers.

Distorted Values

Sports consume
more media coverage,
then Afghanistan,
where volunteer troops
bleed, die
in a hostile country
resisting outsiders,
which assures locals
they can kill each other
as soon as strangers depart.

Why we went in
no longer matters,
an irrational act
invading a country
that made Vietnam
seem sane by comparison.
But capitalists must profit,
first using up old war materials
then selling new war materials.

Since our troops are not draftees
there isn't public resistance
to war far away,
reminding some of us
of the Roman Empire
sending legions abroad
to conquer alien lands,
and when the fighting ended

the troops were forgotten,
because it took weeks to get news
that only affected a few,
friends and families
of distant soldiers,
perhaps leaders of the nation,
while the general public
dealt with greater problems,
day to day existence,
not much different today
despite instant news
from voracious media.

Moments

The last cherry blossoms have fallen.
Only pink leaves remain,
swirling on the tainted ground,
eddies of fading petals
reminding those who notice
of the briefness of beauty.

Troubled Times

Across this troubled land
disasters strike,
hurricanes, tornados, floods,
disruptive terrorism,
yet tourists flock
to New York City
spreading their wealth
to the greedy,
rarely to the needy
suffering foreign invasion
with the bitter acceptance
of all tribulations.

Last Resort

I lost my job
when they hired a kid
at half my salary.
I lost my home
when the bank I bailed out
with my taxes
foreclosed and put us on the street.
Unemployment insurance
will last for a while,
but what then?
I play the lottery,
not believing I'll win,
but fantasizing
about buying a Warhol
or a Senate seat,
but that's no consolation
for my troubles,
just temporary escape.

Apprehension

A beautiful spring day
in New York City,
warm, breezy, balmy,
shoppers carrying their treasures,
tourists photoing everything,
workers on lunch break,
a homeless man scrounging cans,
suddenly a loud bang,
everyone freezes,
some begin to panic,
some turn to run.
All fear the worst.
But traffic keeps moving
and there are no sirens,
so the brief terror passes
until the next event.

Survival Quotient

Once, before cities,
mankind ran, climbed, hid,
from predators,
alarming dangers,
animal alacrity
a vital trait.
Then life became stationary,
sedentary,
and we began to forget
necessary qualities
to prevent untimely demise.
We stopped looking around,
oblivious
to whatever approached.
Spatially challenged
we lost the sense
to move out of the way
of imminent collision.
Consequently,
most of us are only fit
for urban sustainment
completely dependant
on the functions of others
to maintain the system
allowing existence,
leaving many of us
apprehensive
of continuation,
as the nurturing city
rapidly decays.

A Gentler Age II

I watched a man
cackling to himself
as he walked along a city street,
pausing to gesture wildly,
laugh raucously,
possibly listening to rap
on his headset.
First I thought he was happy.
Then I thought he was stoned.
Then I thought he was off his meds.
At least I didn't suspect
he was possessed,
making me wonder why
in a modern society
we let the mad
roam our streets untended.

Recurrence

Despite the advances
in technology
that we take for granted,
some of us
still camp our for days
to get the latest gadget.
And as the Information Age evolves
addicting us
to electronic services
beyond comprehension
a century ago,
civilization
grinds to a halt,
as it always has,
when terrorists assault
the vulnerable public.

To the Fires

Combustible materials
frequently fall
into the wrong hands
and the public burning
of witches, heretics, enemies,
is more like titillation
than education,
as the thrills of spectation
overcome the stench
of human flesh roasting
for real or contrived offenses.

The Natural Way

Most of us
have strong feelings,
get annoyed,
irritated, angry,
lose control
in varying degrees
generally confined
to emotional outbursts,
often resulting
in harsh words,
nasty confrontations,
dreadful violence,
while the simmering desire
to hurt strangers
creates mass destruction,
rooted in nature's
basic harshness
affecting all life.

Sudden Shock

Spontaneous combustion
is frequently blamed
for sudden conflagrations
that consume homes, lives,
cities, nations, aspirations
of a higher good,
turned to ashes
by unknown forces,
surprise enemies,
removing hope
for tranquil continuation.

Distraught

There is no forgiveness
for I have done the deeds
that damaged others
beyond repair,
so there is no relief
for my guilty heart.

Purchase Power

The dance is almost over
for tired feet
that keep shuffling,
despite interruptions,
persistent to attain
the promised land,
denied entry
by callous servants
of the lords of profit,
determined to acquire
every morsel possible
with rapacious talons
for their greedy masters.

Learning Scale

We're not much different
      then the birds,
eating as if
      there's no tomorrow,
unlike some creatures
who store a nest egg
to tide them over,
      unless
nature surprises them,
      wipes out savings
      with sudden storm,
      flash fire,
      flood
natural disasters.
      Some recover.
      Some don't.
Only mankind
ruling the earth
with intelligence,
still hasn't discovered
one does not live
      by brawn alone,
      endlessly tolerates
            bullies,
      the epitome
      of mindless brawn,
            ignored at home,
            school,
      as inferior minds

torment
 mental betters.
But what should we expect
from a demented species
that concocts
 unnatural acts
that destroy the nest eggs
of hard working creatures
 forced to endure
 inflictions
from man and nature.

Transactions

Tourists stream through Bryant Park
intent on destinations
cultural, culinary,
diverse entertainment,
mostly shopping,
acquiring goods
too costly at home,
pursuit of a bargain
once a typical quest
of Americans abroad.
Now prosperous foreigners
rummage our land
as we once rummaged theirs.

Renewal

Spring is a sensory eruption,
delighting in its awakening
those starved by winter starkness.
Magnolias briefly bloom
dazzling the eyes
with elegant beauty,
intoxicating the nose
with nature's finest scent,
never duplicated
in contrived laboratories.
Forsythia bright cheer leader
urging on iris, daffodil, hyacinth,
to enthrall with the palette
of seasonal colors
enriching those
who look.

Home is Where....

Our masters no longer reside
in fortified castles
that dominate the lives
of all who dwell nearby,
nor in grandiose palaces
that dazzle the eyes
of servants, the envious,
seeking crumbs
from tables of abundance,
not in great mansions
that people pass with respect,
curious about hidden lives
sheltered by prosperity
far removed from daily toil
that burdens most of us.
Now our masters live
on great estates
removed from public scrutiny,
wealth purchasing privacy
as they enjoy the benefits
of accumulated privilege.

Hi-Tech Times

In every hand an Iphone
owner busy
talking, texting,
an innovative comfort
allowing constant communication
anytime, anywhere
subject to interruption
of cellular service,
yet more and more prevalent
facilitating contact,
no matter what the content.

Intrusion

Forced entry
 into caves, mud huts,
castles, log cabins, condos,
has been a constant,
despite best efforts
of self defense,
violent penetration
usually resulting
in looting, rape, slaughter,
violation
of the dwelling,
yet more survive
in modern times,
courtesy of
better law and order.

Diminishing Return

I do not know
what point in time
mankind perceived
there was a future
and made efforts
to perpetuate the race.
Despite vaunted intelligence
that gave us
the Age of Reason
and much later
the Information Age,
we never developed
the Age of Wisdom.
Instead of evolving
to become caretakers
of our only habitat
the peculiar planet
that sustains our lives,
we remain depredators
devouring as much as we can,
regardless of the harm
to the balance of nature,
destroying carelessly,
purposelessly,
what should sustain the future,
leaving little hope
that good sense will prevail
and we will someday learn
to be custodians
of Mother Earth.

Fulminating

Aspirations leaking
anemic fluid
bleed away
the last configuration
of delusive expectations,
finally resigned
to dwindling returns,
hope diminished
by resentful particles
waiting to inflict
conflagration
on the unwary.

Tourist Season

I sit in a city park
on a hot summer day
watching people pass,
most of them tired,
bedraggled, still surprised
at New York weather,
led by travel agents
to expect a balmy climate,
although without singing peasants,
where they could spend their euros
in complete comfort,
while finding bargains
from obliging natives.

Convulsions

Your changing face, city,
features past remembrance
streets I have known, walked,
proclaiming me a stranger
bewildered in a foreign land
bereft of landmarks,
familiar places departed,
buildings where friends resided,
stores where I shopped,
restaurants where I dined,
all gone, as if never were.
No reminders remain
who lived, worked, played, loved,
no placards, signs, memorials,
only trace recollections
of another life.

City Waste

A man lies in a doorway,
dead, drunk, diseased,
no one stops to look
averting eyes
from distasteful sight,
the same people
who in accident, emergency,
rush to help others,
this urban casualty
beyond recognition
of middle-class sensibilities.

A Dubious Future

Spring rejuvenates
minds and bodies
weary of the cold,
the daffodils and iris
delight and delude us
for all is not well.
The unrestrained attack
on our habitat
toxifies the air
until one day
we run out of gasps.
The burdens of war,
poverty, disease,
divert us from the threat
to continued respiration
as we lurch clumsily
in the garden of existence.

Crime Against Humanity

New York City homeless shelters
reached record numbers,
fifty thousand people,
twenty thousand children,
abandoned by a callous city
unrepresented by the system
since they don't legally reside
in elected official's districts,
so their only advocates
are not-for-profit organizations
more concerned with litigation
than the desperate needs
of suffering victims,
men, women, children.

Shades of Prosperity

Spring in the city,
flowers blooming,
trees already fully green,
some benevolent days
despite climate change,
and while many New Yorkers
struggle to survive
tourists flaunt their wealth
lugging expensive shopping bags,
poking expensive cameras
into anything that moves,
not yet vulture-like
feeding on dead carrion,
more undertaker-like
appraising future customers.

Abandonment

Some of us moved
as far as possible
from nature,
surrounding ourselves
with illusory protection
of stone, concrete, steel,
until the occasional tree
is rarely noticed
in the daily pursuit
of livelihood.

Vacationing

Groups of tourists
travel together
for comfort, reassurance
from the perils of the road,
secure with others
who speak the same language,
euros, cameras, bargains,
always eager for the sights
through the lens darkly,
never fully relaxed
until they reach the safety
of expensive hotel rooms.

Duality

Foreign threats
multiply
as fast as
domestic threats,
combining
to disrupt
peaceful existence.

Crumbling Ramparts

The cold war ended
without mutual destruction
some sense retained
to contain the madness.
Religious war
creeps across the world
as a super power
disintegrates
as it consumes its wealth
on super weapons,
completely useless
against inexpensive,
home-grown terrorism.

Onset

I survived another winter,
fortunately not too chilling
and with a sudden rush
spring invaded the city
with platoons of magnolias,
companies of cherry trees,
battalions of forsythia,
regiments of dogwood,
endless armies of daffodils,
in an undeclared war
on urban sensibilities.

Purchase Power II

Patrons of the art world
bid at auction
competing for masterworks
against rival appetites,
efforts rewarded
by acquisition,
applause of the crowd
for record prices,
feelings of possession
of a treasured item
won in economic battle,
soon to molder unnoticed
on crowded walls,
denuded of satisfaction.

Commodity Market

Pretentious art galleries
intimidate people
cowed by expensive surroundings,
expensive paintings,
condescending salesmen
except to buyers
who if wealthy enough
look down at everyone
spuriously confident
in the power of the purse.

Lest We Forget

Terrorist threats
become a constant
in religious war
against the haves,
since poverty pockets
are rarely attacked
by considerate suiciders,
trying to detonate
at public events,
significant landmarks,
targets of opportunity
with enough value,
shattering our illusion
of secure existence
in a violent blast
ending tranquility.

Velocity

In a very short time
we left horses behind
using motor power
to get from place to place.
Although we moved faster,
we didn't get smarter
and used motor power
to kill more and more of us,
as well as the land
that nurtured us.
If the past is a pattern,
we'll move so fast
we'll leave nothing behind.

Recurrence II

Commotion
attracts a crowd,
some hoping for disaster
to feast on blood, suffering,
but most are horrified
sensitive to the agonies
of innocent victims,
occurring more often
in our troubled land.

Suffusion

We no longer rise at dawn,
do the chores, till the fields,
yet we still suffer
indignities
that nature provides,
flood, drought, tornado,
disrupting fragile lives
that sit up late each night
glued to the television set
accepting programming
determining behavior,
social, economic,
moral, political,
until we no longer know
right from wrong.

Losses

Spring migration
and the warblers head north
passing through Bryant Park
mostly unnoticed,
unaware
that climate change,
loss of forest,
concrete,
will further reduce
diminishing habitat.

Ongoing Events

Human events
      perplex
       most of us,
who care to comprehend
that things happen
with or without
      consent,
       affecting us
      differently,
      some thriving,
      some surviving,
      some perishing,
      determined
             by fate,
coincidence,
      ill luck,
human contrivances
supplementing
nature's afflictions.

Substitute

In the city
tourists come and go
cameras poised,
eyes alert seeking
targets of opportunity,
photos more important
than personal experience,
so they can be posted
for public consumption
on Facebook… other
social media sites
to be admired, shared,
appreciated
by those who can't afford
foreign travel,
but get almost as much
from colorful photos
as those who went abroad.

Purpose

A rainstorm swept the city,
thunder, lightning, flooding,
keeping many indoors
except first responders
risking all
regardless of conditions,
as tourists
urgent to shop
are relentless
in pursuit of bargains,
despite interference
by man or nature.

Troubled Times II

Feelings of dread
possess many
who seek escape,
forgetfulness
from the angst
real, imagined,
sheltering in drugs,
sex, mad rampages.
Constructive solutions
rare events
in an overburdened land
of constant demand,
security available
for purchase by the rich.

Noon

Lunchtime in the city
and the employed
leave their warrens,
a few to posh restaurants
most to ready-made,
or sandwiches,
some go to the nearest park
enjoying the illusion
of urban outdoors
offering relief,
however brief
from encroaching concrete.

Confused State

Before radios, tv,
the internet,
public anger
was easily aroused
by cunning newspapers
turned on targets
selected by government,
special interests,
predictable behavior
making manipulation easy.
Endless quantities of information
dilute the call to action
and fewer and fewer summons
evoke a response,
circuits too overloaded,
with confusing transmissions.

Congestion

Bicycles begin to clog the streets
competing with combustion engines
to get from place to place
in a challenging environment
originally evolved
from foot and horse traffic,
design improvised
until modern times,
when it was too late
for urban adaptation
of the automobile.

Benefits of the Internet

The more we learn
at the punch of a button
the more we can do
with knowledge acquired,
as access to all
allows unrestricted freedom
to use information
for good, evil, diversion,
creating an ethics question
of right and wrong
to letting anyone
do what they want,
including terrorism,
as we wonder
who will control the genie
let out of the bottle.

Paranoia

Symptoms of persecution
are distressingly normal
in a deceptive society
constantly untrustworthy,
where the lies, big and small
confuse the information flow
on the electronic highways,
so far removed from verification
we can no longer separate
fact from fiction.

Know Thy Oppressors

After Congress displayed
indifference to the suffering
inflicted on the people
because they would not agree
on fiscal policy,
the loss of jobs, services,
further weakened
a staggering nation
already reeling
from economic woes,
making us yearn
for old-fashioned corruption
rather than basic greed,
eroding the fabric
of a troubled land.

Odds Are

Double or nothing
always seems a daring bet.
Unless you have nothing to lose,
and if the value of double
is not life changing
the rush is ephemeral,
the reward minimal,
results concluding
with smug victory,
resentful defeat.

Assault Team

Traffic clogs the roads
cars, buses, taxis, trucks,
many driving recklessly,
all emitting toxins
courtesy of
the oil industry
more concerned with profit
than the human condition,
survival of the earth
a matter of indifference,
as long as the wealthy
maintain their comforts.

The Democratic Process

Signs of decay
pour from the pores
of stricken society,
assisted by servants
who toil for the prosperous
uncaring if they consume
the vulnerable people,
as long as they preserve
the wealth of their masters.

Similarity

Everyone
is starting to look
like everyone else,
homogeneity
provided by tv,
increasing protein,
similar attire,
identical homes,
at least for those
who can afford homes,
individualism
definitely receding,
conquered by stereotypes.

Erratic Days

We can no longer rely
on stable weather patterns,
with rapid temperature flux,
extremely powerful storms,
too much or too little rain,
all disrupting acclimatization,
due to the shock of climate change.

Korean Understudies

Huge armies
armed with powerful weapons
capable of great destruction,
face each other, kept apart
by an imaginary line
arbitrarily designed
to separate two enemies,
supported by two rivals,
avoiding direct warfare,
substituting tensions
for violent confrontation
by volatile proxies.

Public Service

City congestion
puts us closer together,
detonation unavoidable.
Forces of law and order
patrol, pursue, persecute,
seem to serve the people,
as long as it doesn't distract
from protection of property,
security for the wealthy.

Distress Signal

Crumpled dreams
resonate across the land
in troubled homes,
expectations washed away
by storm, greed, stupidity,
and as hope flickers
for the fading promise
of a decent life,
the halls of power
are inattentive
to those in need.

Grandeur Passing

Uncle Sam represents
the image of a nation,
although Old Sam
is a bit worn down these days
with all the threats
that multiply daily
for our besieged people.
Yet we shouldn't forget
Uncle Walt,
(and I don't mean Disney, dodos.)
who sang of America
with innocence, abandon,
while spiritually ill
at the horrors of war
he saw in broken bodies
in Civil War hospitals,
that never persuaded him
to renounce the ideals
that sustained democracy.

Occurrences

Natural disasters
are different
from man-made disasters
that should always be regretted
by people of intelligence,
people of compassion,
since misguided actions
might have been averted,
while nature's fury
is beyond control.

Undue Extremes

In the twilight of cities
citizens of disdain
sneer at the sufferings
of those beneath them,
flaunting their wealth
in arrogant displays
of acquisitions,
Picassos, Rothkos, Warhols,
while many struggle
for food and shelter.

Glibness Revealed

Subtle threads of deception
weave through the fraying fabric
of a troubled land,
as self-righteous leaders,
vowing their sincerity,
proclaim opposition
to laws that help the people,
opting instead
to serve the interests
of the anonymous wealthy.

Evolutionary Chance

Survival is determined
by luck, chance, coincidence,
as we huddle in comfort
in artificial enclaves,
no longer remembering
the ardor of hunting/gathering,
terror of the night,
too brief life spans
that somehow existed long enough
to build great cities
where millions dwell
in temporary safety.

Contributions

Eruptions of anger
poison the atmosphere
already toxic
from artificial infusions
of industrial corrosives
polluting us
beyond redemption,
draining hopes
past resuscitation,
emergency services
insufficient
to halt the tide
of fateful incursions.

Non-Redemption

A person of intelligence
with a developed moral sense
cannot easily forget
pain caused to others
by ignorance, neglect,
whatever the reason
the suffering we cause
continues to affect
the lives of others,
regardless of regret
we cannot obliterate
sins of commission,
sins of omission.

Guilt Strains

The commission of a crime
that hurts someone
cannot be atoned for,
since the harm is done
and any reparation
whether payment, prison,
does not eradicate
the damage suffered
by innocent victims.

Last Shot

Stocks rise to record highs
luring some to invest,
hoping to make money
in a distressed economy,
since they don't know what to do
in the crumbling world
erasing the middle-class
as a factor in the future,
the last remnants tainting the system
to redeem drastic losses
that shattered life styles,
now departed, leaving dread
that former prosperity
will never come again.

Survival Trait

We all have a breaking point,
mental, physical, emotional,
that we cannot go beyond,
reaching our limits,
crumbling by the wayside
unable to continue
supporting our loved ones,
recovering from illness,
remaining sane in a world gone mad,
the only consolation
pride in perseverance
surpassing expectations,
inspiring others
in the struggle to endure
constant tribulations.

Unbelief

As religion fades
as a vital force
in the indulgent West
the volume of disasters,
man made, natural,
multiply like plague
inflicted on the greedy
and only the doubtful prospect
of a genuine miracle
may arrive in time
to save us from destruction.

Shopping Spree II

TV and the internet
send slick ads
to conditioned audiences
to buy costly goods,
cars, clothes, jewelry,
tempting us beyond resistance
to acquire desired treasures
and we loyally comply,
responding to our nurturers
in the last indulgences
before crippling poverty.

Endless Struggle

Surges of crime,
violence, terror,
seem to overwhelm
less conspicuous
forces of goodness
that must always strive
so they can survive
the onslaught of evil.

Confused Values

Terrorists plot and scheme
to destroy their enemies
who are protected part-time
by intelligence agencies
that may lack the intelligence
to prevent attacks,
but sometimes capture the perps,
who are treated as humans,
at least in America,
given fair trials,
rights guaranteed
as much as any citizen,
and if found guilty
sentenced to prison,
food, shelter, clothing,
medical services
denied to many of our people,
all at public expense
paid for with the taxes
from the same folk
they tried to destroy.

Large Hive

No matter how far
you fly in search of pollen
you're unlikely to meet
another friendly bee,
in the big field.

Advances

Access to the internet
allows anyone,
democratically,
to learn how
in convenient tutorials
to make weapons of mass destruction,
chemical, biological, nuclear,
only restricted by funding,
since money buys anything.
So the blueprint to destroy the world
is readily available
and sooner or later
a lunatic loner
will overcome the obstacles
that prevent acquisition
of dangerous substances
and unleash them
on the unprepared public.

First Responders

Sudden detonations
instantly terrify
most people,
sending them scurrying
away for safety,
while first responders
automatically
run the other way
into danger,
often without knowing
what they'll confront,
personal cares suppressed
in brave determination
to help others.

Unperceptive

Tensions build,
emotions smolder,
sudden outbursts
surprise the unwary,
who should be more aware
of feelings of discontent
that lead to assault.

Violations

Each day the news
reveals new horrors,
crime, murder, terrorism,
until we are besieged
with tragedy, suffering,
and we painfully assume
we have seen it all,
but the human monster
never sleeps,
contriving new assaults
on strained systems
that have no choice
but to accept
the unacceptable.

Momentary Distractions

Disruptions
to the public well-being,
accidents, murders, terror,
do not prevent
most of us
from getting up
the next day,
going about our business
as if disaster
never happened.

Tantrum

Yelling and screaming
are symptoms of anger,
impatience, resentment,
loss of control
an indication
of dissatisfaction
with the status quo.

Urban Extension

As we deplete
the natural environment,
the cities grow larger
absorbing more refugees
from untillable land,
compelled,
without choice,
to urban adaptation,
dwindling existence.

Hazardous Duty

First responders
are mostly forgotten
except in a crisis,
the moment of need
when against all logic
they bravely rush
into threats of death
to rescue strangers,
who suddenly appreciate
the dangers faced
in recurring hazards.

No Storm Warning

Harmony is interrupted
by surprise detonations
of emotional outrage
at the real, imagined,
offenses suddenly viral
infecting those exposed
to unexpected fury,
difficult to sooth.

Chance

As much as we try
to avoid unpleasantness,
disaster strikes,
flood, drought, plague,
Mongol invasion,
disrupting plans
for a great evening,
circumstances deciding
who survives,
who perishes.

Impelled

Urgency,
a crisis state,
propagates stress,
only relieved
by accomplishment,
or failure
to communicate
desired outcomes.

Class Order

The life of a city,
as long as it is vital,
is building and rebuilding
with desperate streets
beyond condolence
devouring shattered hopes
of persecuted children
denied escape
from holocaust poverty,
while the prosperous,
serenely insulated
from the angst
of finding daily bread
securely wend their way
through urban comforts,
oblivious, uncaring
that the fears of the poor
consume their future.

Reverberations

Accident, injury, death,
interruptions,
often unexpected
in daily agenda,
home, work, play,
expectations arrested,
security shattering
remaining hopes
for rapid recovery.

At Play

We spend more on recreation
than on education,
so we'll have a lot of fun
until we're too dumb
to repair our toys.

Westward Ho

Once we went west
for gold, gain, god,
whatever we could find
in untamed wilderness.
Then many stayed
working the land
and built a country.
With nowhere left to go
for restless wanderers,
space forgotten,
the absence of frontiers
rebirthed irate congestion
without room to dissipate,
breeding conflict
on a narrowing globe.
Yet hope not extinguished
for extraterrestrial
exploration, colonization
before detonation.

Fire Drill

The announcement informs
it is only a test
and hundreds of people
evacuate orderly,
chatting, joking, relaxed,
glad to be out of the office
even for a short while,
few realizing
that a genuine event
will be chaotic,
terrifying.

Disruption

Visitors stroll
casually through the park,
most ignoring the flowers,
birds, greenery,
intent on destinations
more important
than enjoyment,
nature's respite.
All is calm
until yells, screams,
the sounds of conflict
alert passersby,
something has gone wrong
in this temporary refuge.

Gary Beck has spent most of his adult life as a theater director and worked as an art dealer when he couldn't earn a living in the theater. He has also been a tennis pro, a ditch digger and a salvage diver. His original plays and translations of Moliere, Aristophanes and Sophocles have been produced Off Broadway. His poetry, fiction and essays have appeared in hundreds of literary magazines and his published books include 30 poetry collections, 12 novels, 3 short story collections, 1 collection of essays and 3 books of plays. Published poetry books include: *Dawn in Cities, Assault on Nature, Songs of a Clerk, Civilized Ways, Displays, Perceptions, Fault Lines, Tremors, Perturbations, Rude Awakenings, The Remission of Order, Contusions* and *Desperate Seeker* (Winter Goose Publishing. Forthcoming: *Learning Curve*). *Earth Links, Too Harsh For Pastels, Severance, Redemption Value, Fractional Disorder* and *Disruptions* (Cyberwit Publishing. Forthcoming: Ignition Point). His novels include *Extreme Change* (Winter Goose Publishing). *State of Rage and Wavelength* (Cyberwit Publishing. Forthcoming: *Protective Agency and Obsess*). His short story collections include: *A Glimpse of Youth* (Sweatshoppe Publications). *Now I Accuse and other stories* (Winter Goose Publishing) and *Dogs Don't Send Flowers and other stories* (Wordcatcher Publishing). *Collected Essays of Gary Beck* (Cyberwit Publishing). *The Big Match and other one act plays* (Wordcatcher Publishing). *Collected Plays of Gary Beck Volume 1* and *Plays of Aristophanes* translated, then directed by Gary Beck (Cyberwit Publishing. Forthcoming: *Collected Plays of Gary Beck Volume II*). Gary lives in New York City.

www.ingramcontent.com/pod-product-compliance
Lightning Source LLC
LaVergne TN
LVHW011303210726

843509LV00016B/694